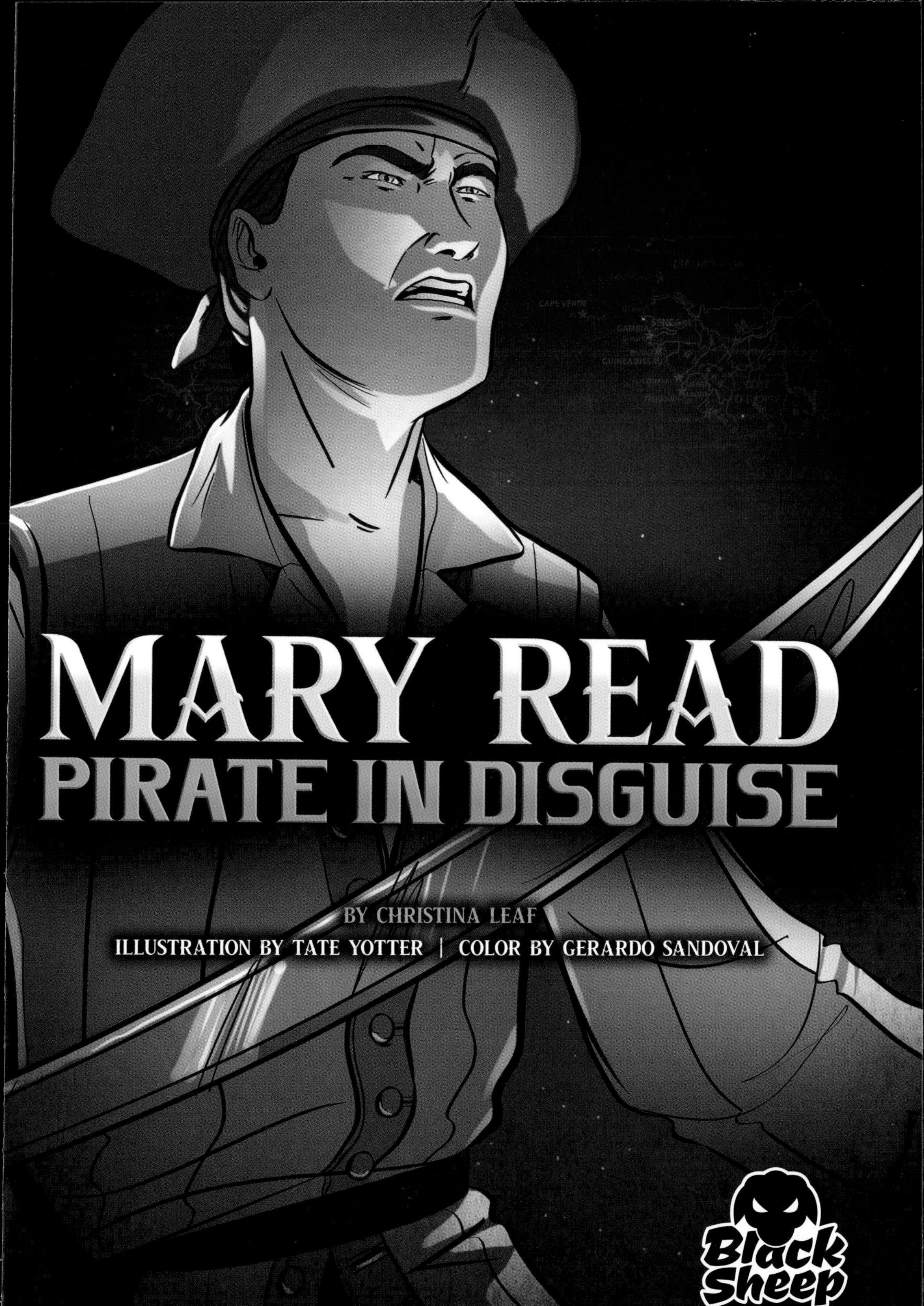

MARY READ
PIRATE IN DISGUISE

BY CHRISTINA LEAF

ILLUSTRATION BY TATE YOTTER | COLOR BY GERARDO SANDOVAL

Black Sheep

BELLWETHER MEDIA • MINNEAPOLIS, MN

STRAY FROM REGULAR READS
WITH BLACK SHEEP BOOKS.
FEEL A RUSH WITH EVERY READ!

This edition first published in 2021 by Bellwether Media, Inc.

No part of this publication may be reproduced in whole or in part without written permission of the publisher.
For information regarding permission, write to Bellwether Media, Inc., Attention: Permissions Department,
6012 Blue Circle Drive, Minnetonka, MN 55343.

Library of Congress Cataloging-in-Publication Data

Names: Leaf, Christina, author.
Title: Mary Read : pirate in disguise / Christina Leaf.
Description: Minneapolis : Bellwether Media, 2021. | Series: Black sheep : pirate tales | Includes bibliographical references
    and index. | Audience: Ages 7-13 | Audience: Grades 4-6 | Summary: "Exciting illustrations follow events in the life
    of Mary Read. The combination of brightly colored panels and leveled text is intended for students in grades 3 through
    8"–Provided by publisher.
Identifiers: LCCN 2020017781 (print) | LCCN 2020017782 (ebook) | ISBN 9781644873045 (library binding) | ISBN
    9781681038438 (paperback) | ISBN 9781681037615 (ebook)
Subjects: LCSH: Read, Mary, -1720?–Juvenile literature. | Women pirates–Caribbean Sea–Biography–Juvenile literature. |
    Pirates–Caribbean Sea–Biography–Juvenile literature.
Classification: LCC G537.R43 L43 2021 (print) | LCC G537.R43 (ebook) | DDC 910.4/5 [B]–dc23
LC record available at https://lccn.loc.gov/2020017781
LC ebook record available at https://lccn.loc.gov/2020017782

Editor: Betsy Rathburn   Designer: Andrea Schneider

Printed in the United States of America, North Mankato, MN.

TABLE OF CONTENTS

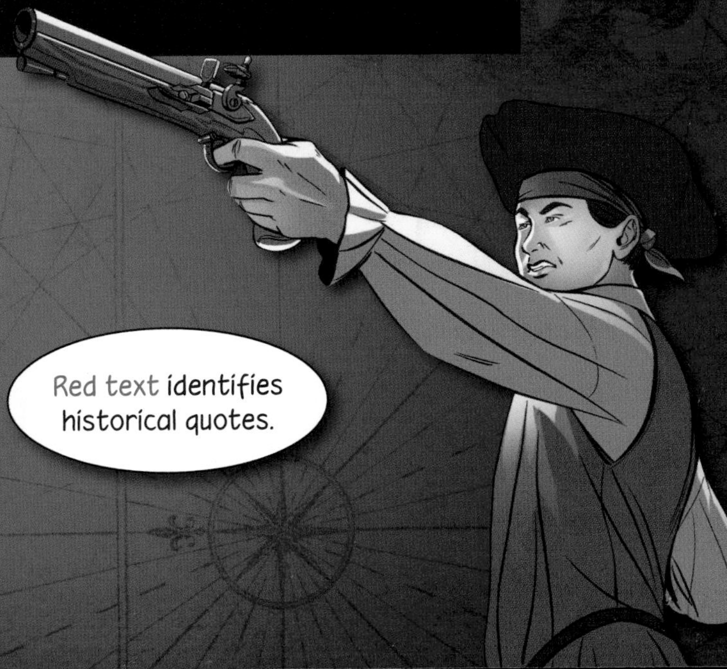

Red text identifies historical quotes.

In Disguise

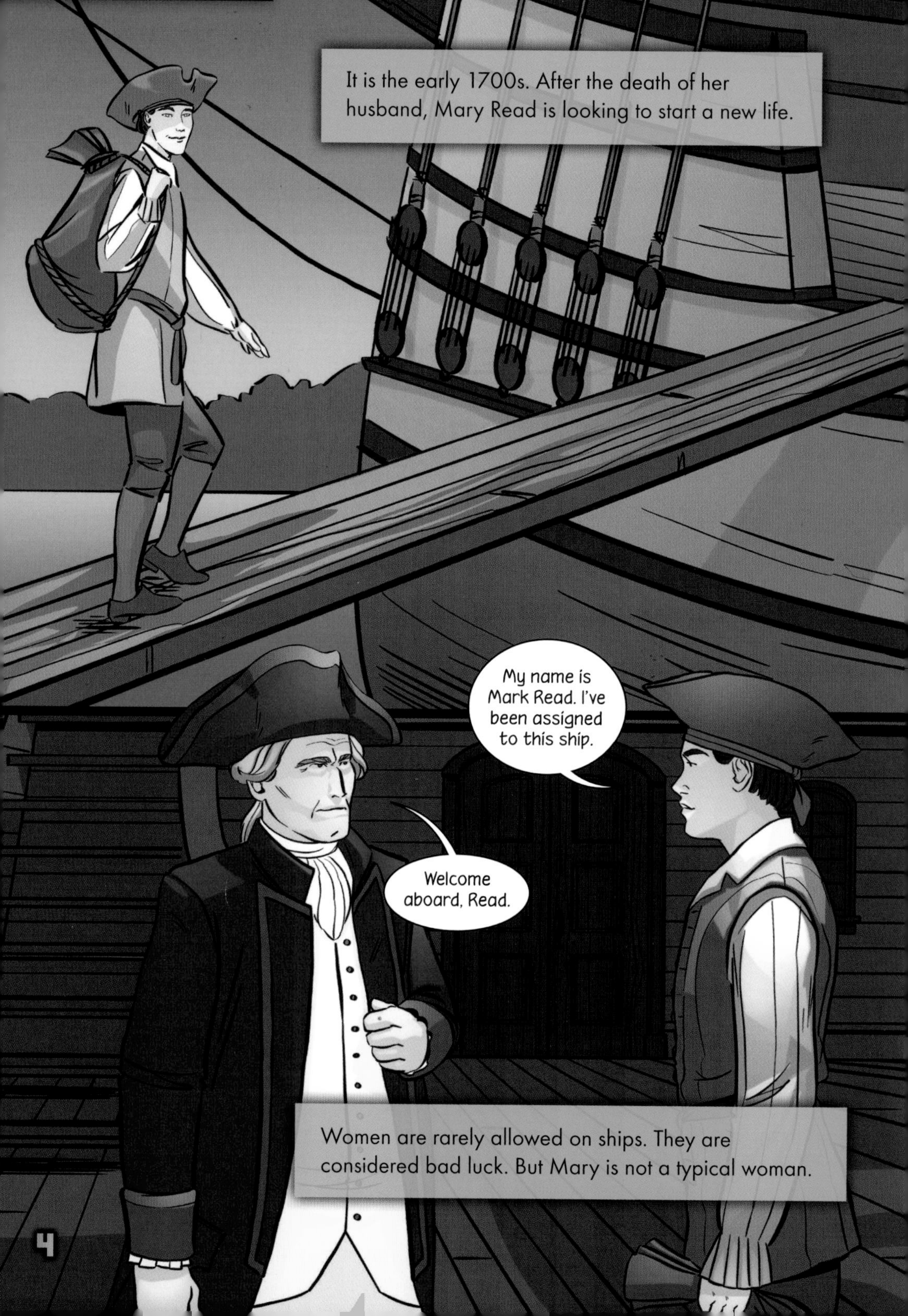
It is the early 1700s. After the death of her husband, Mary Read is looking to start a new life.
My name is Mark Read. I've been assigned to this ship.
Welcome aboard, Read.
Women are rarely allowed on ships. They are considered bad luck. But Mary is not a typical woman.

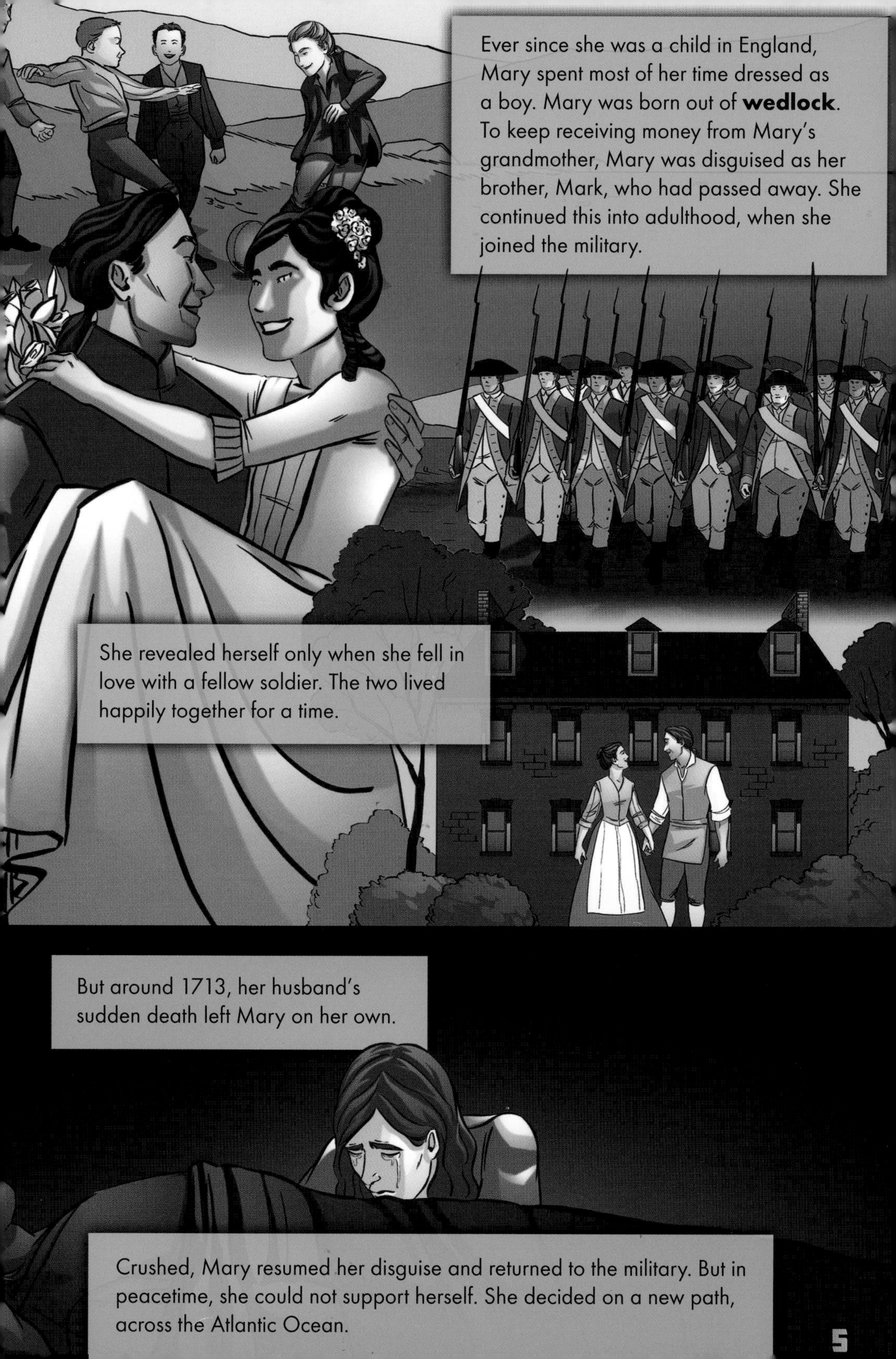
Ever since she was a child in England, Mary spent most of her time dressed as a boy. Mary was born out of **wedlock**. To keep receiving money from Mary's grandmother, Mary was disguised as her brother, Mark, who had passed away. She continued this into adulthood, when she joined the military.
She revealed herself only when she fell in love with a fellow soldier. The two lived happily together for a time.
But around 1713, her husband's sudden death left Mary on her own.
Crushed, Mary resumed her disguise and returned to the military. But in peacetime, she could not support herself. She decided on a new path, across the Atlantic Ocean.

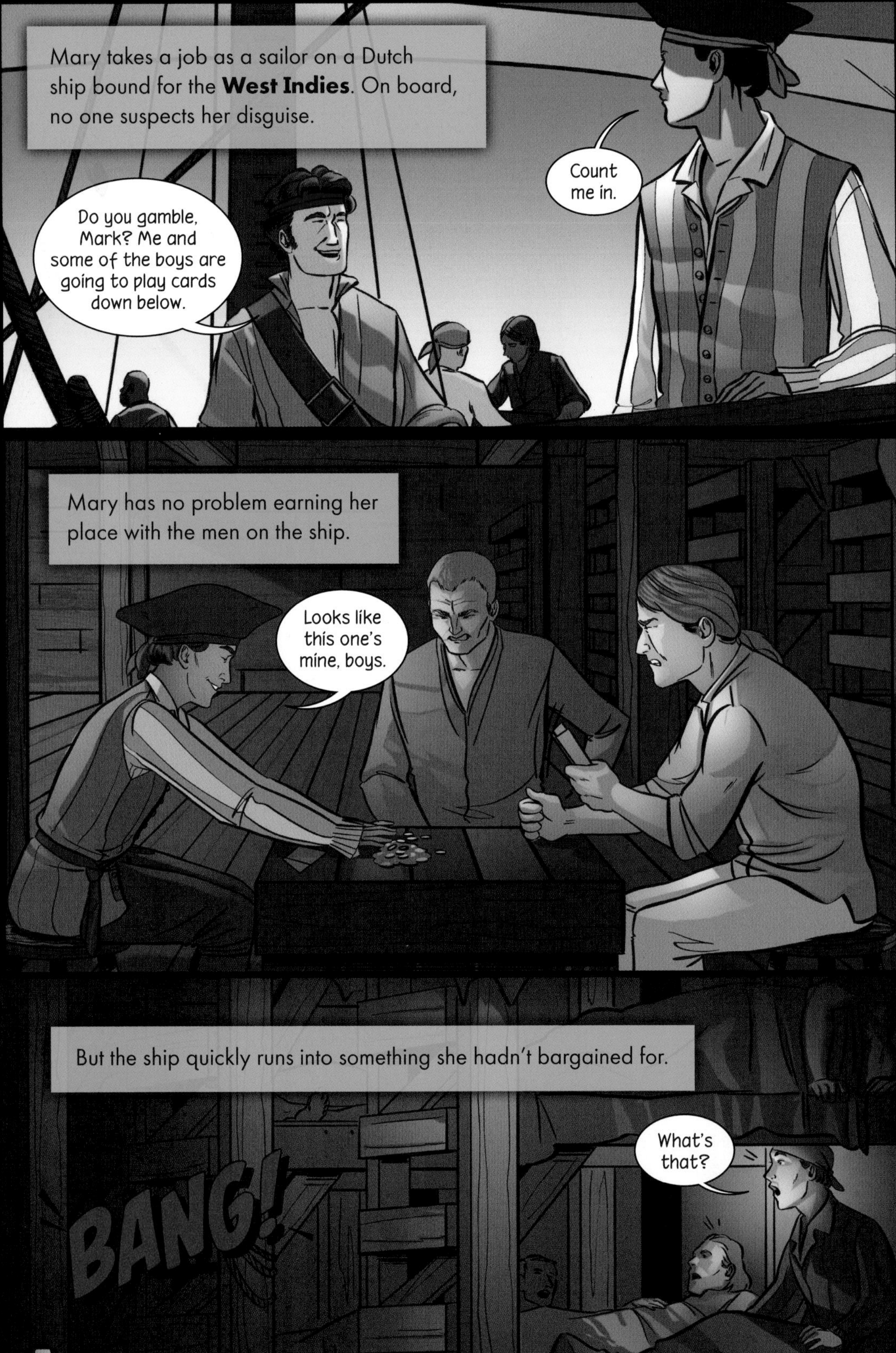
Mary takes a job as a sailor on a Dutch ship bound for the **West Indies**. On board, no one suspects her disguise.
Do you gamble, Mark? Me and some of the boys are going to play cards down below.
Count me in.
Mary has no problem earning her place with the men on the ship.
Looks like this one's mine, boys.
But the ship quickly runs into something she hadn't bargained for.
BANG!
What's that?

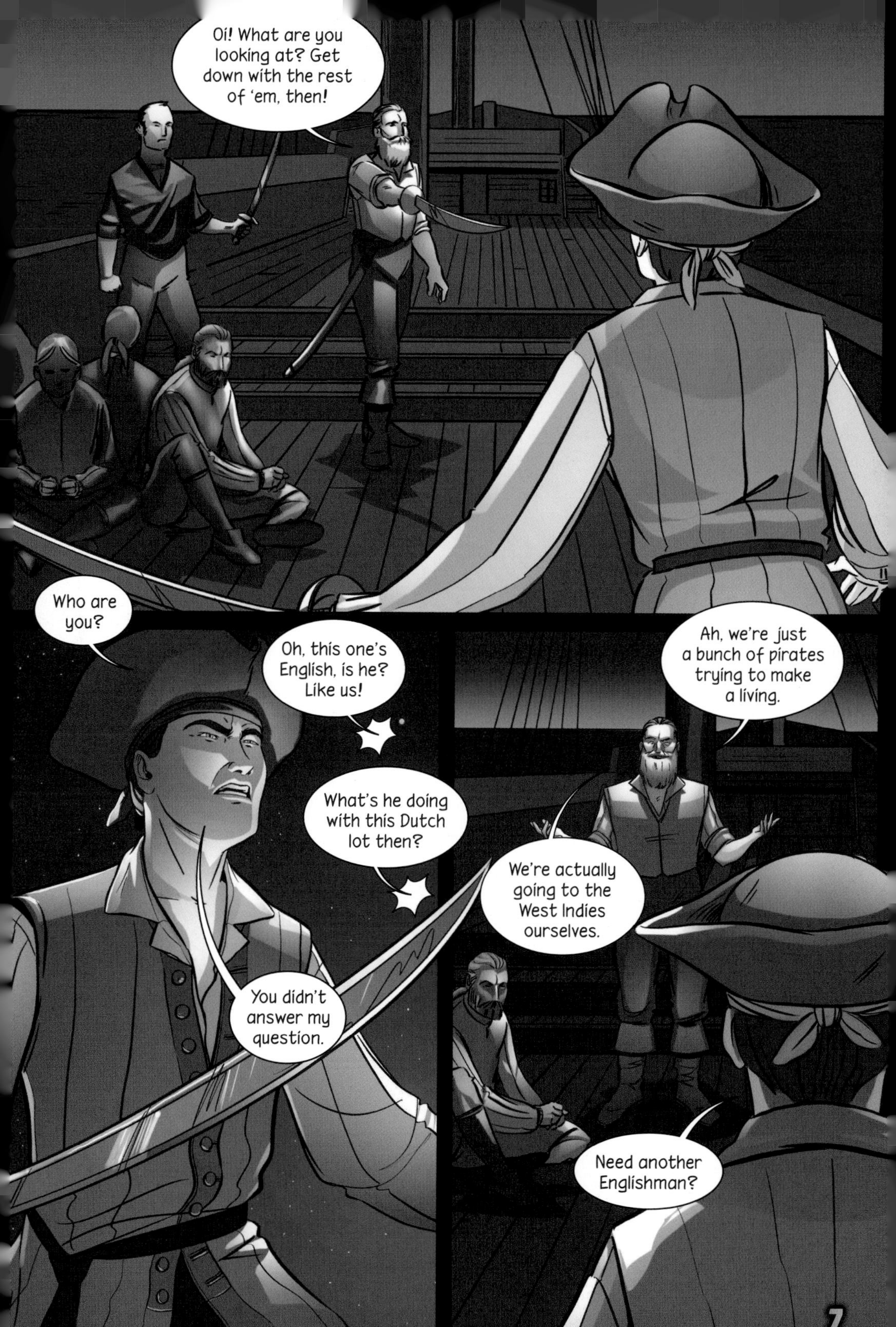
Oi! What are you looking at? Get down with the rest of 'em, then!
Who are you?
Oh, this one's English, is he? Like us!
What's he doing with this Dutch lot then?
You didn't answer my question.
Ah, we're just a bunch of pirates trying to make a living.
We're actually going to the West Indies ourselves.
Need another Englishman?

A Pirate's Life

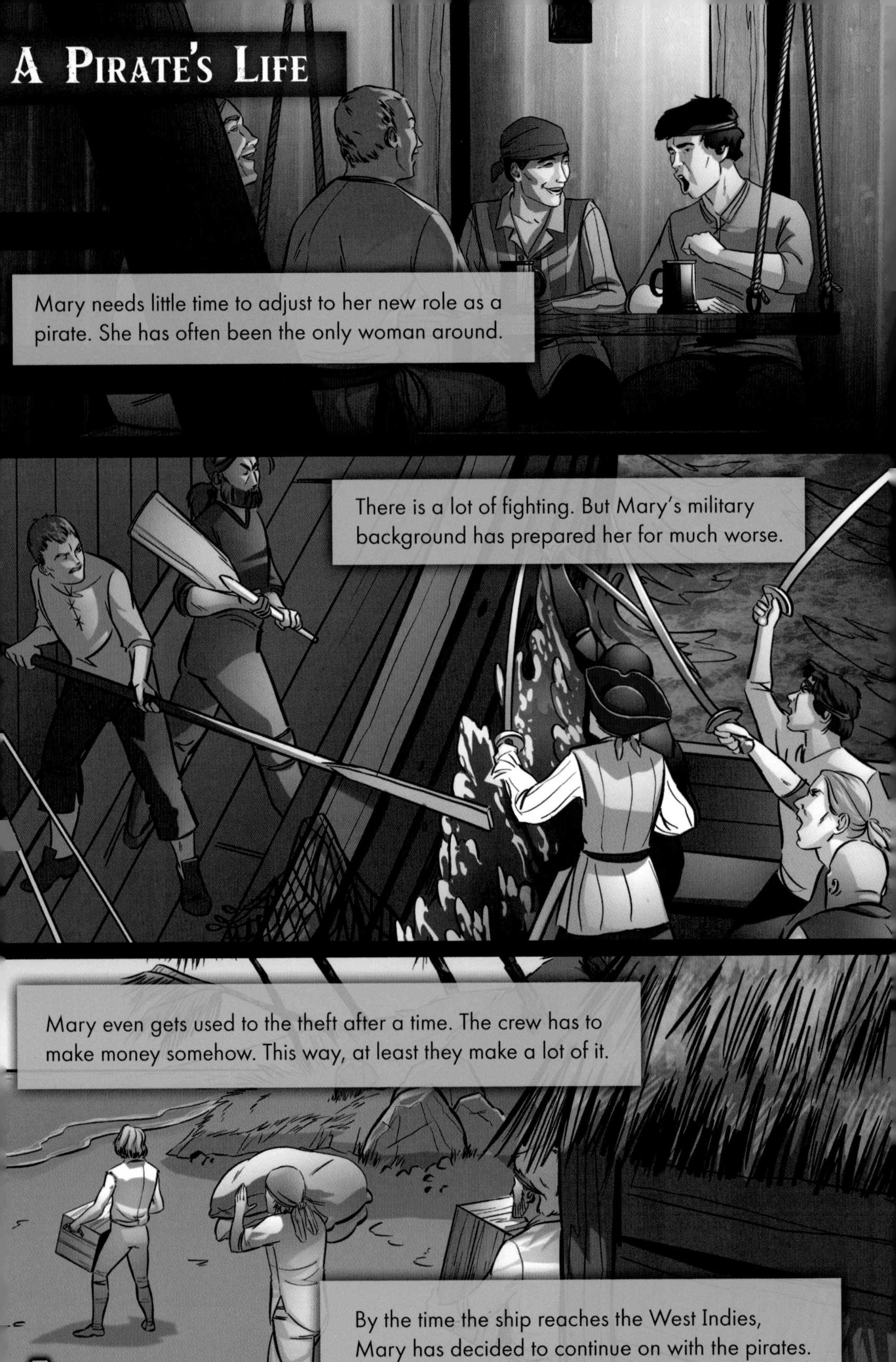
Mary needs little time to adjust to her new role as a pirate. She has often been the only woman around.
There is a lot of fighting. But Mary's military background has prepared her for much worse.
Mary even gets used to the theft after a time. The crew has to make money somehow. This way, at least they make a lot of it.
By the time the ship reaches the West Indies, Mary has decided to continue on with the pirates.

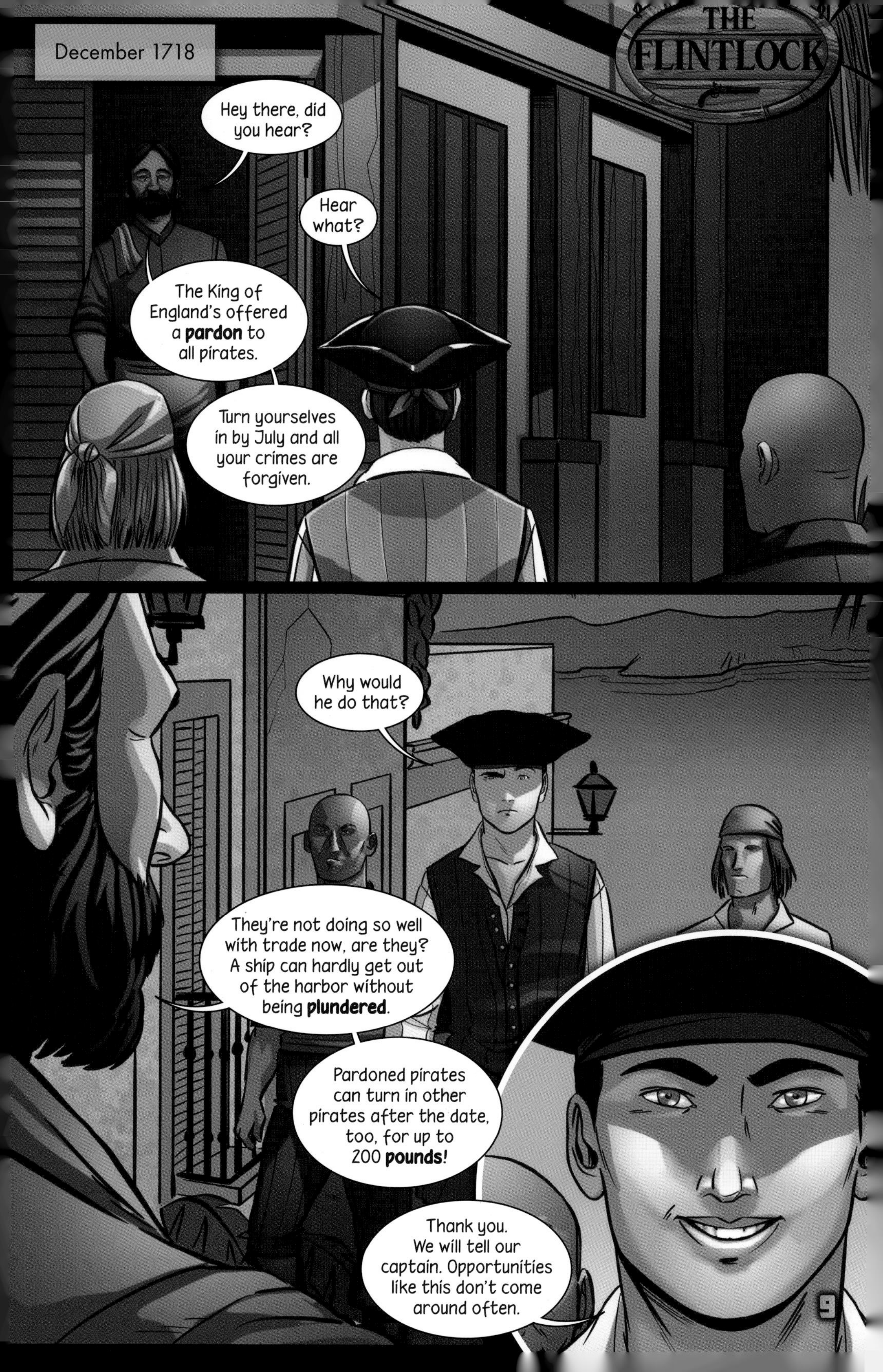
December 1718
THE FLINTLOCK
Hey there, did you hear?
Hear what?
The King of England's offered a **pardon** to all pirates.
Turn yourselves in by July and all your crimes are forgiven.
Why would he do that?
They're not doing so well with trade now, are they? A ship can hardly get out of the harbor without being **plundered**.
Pardoned pirates can turn in other pirates after the date, too, for up to 200 **pounds**!
Thank you. We will tell our captain. Opportunities like this don't come around often.

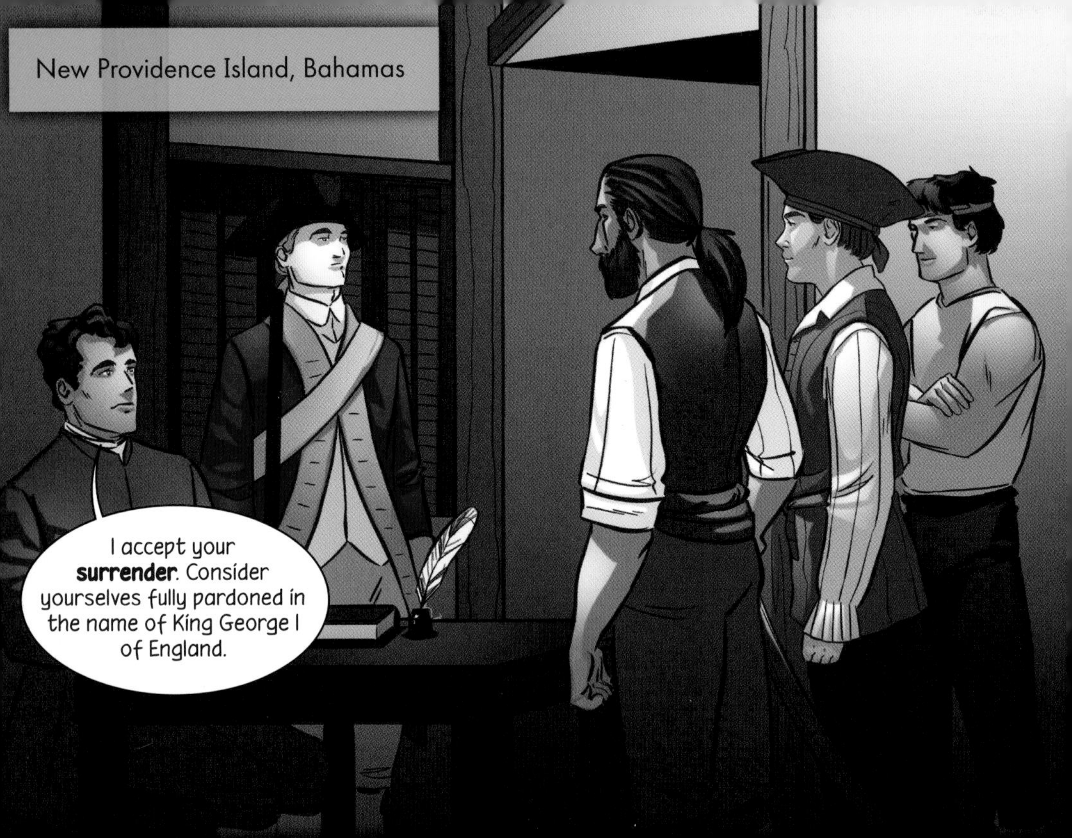
New Providence Island, Bahamas
I accept your **surrender**. Consider yourselves fully pardoned in the name of King George I of England.

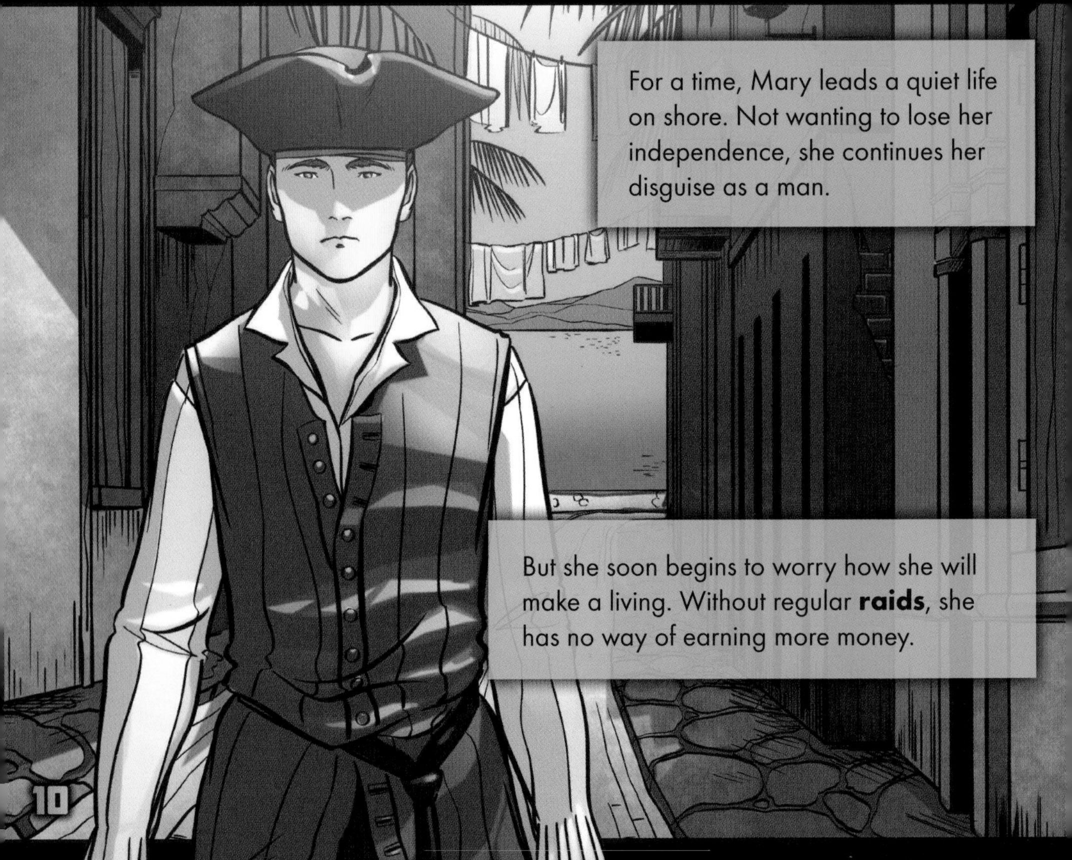
For a time, Mary leads a quiet life on shore. Not wanting to lose her independence, she continues her disguise as a man.
But she soon begins to worry how she will make a living. Without regular **raids**, she has no way of earning more money.

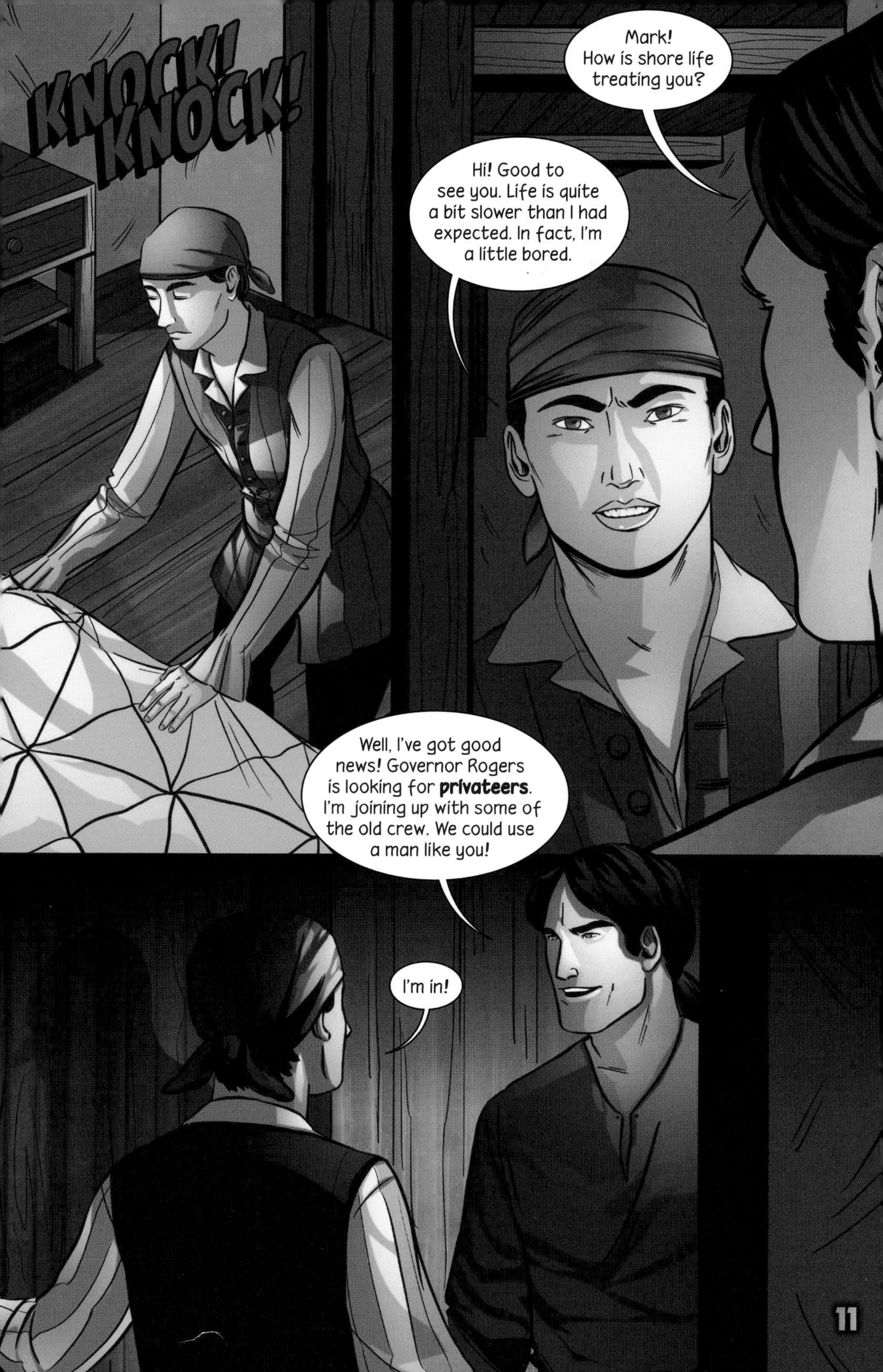
KNOCK! KNOCK!
Mark! How is shore life treating you?
Hi! Good to see you. Life is quite a bit slower than I had expected. In fact, I'm a little bored.
Well, I've got good news! Governor Rogers is looking for **privateers**. I'm joining up with some of the old crew. We could use a man like you!
I'm in!

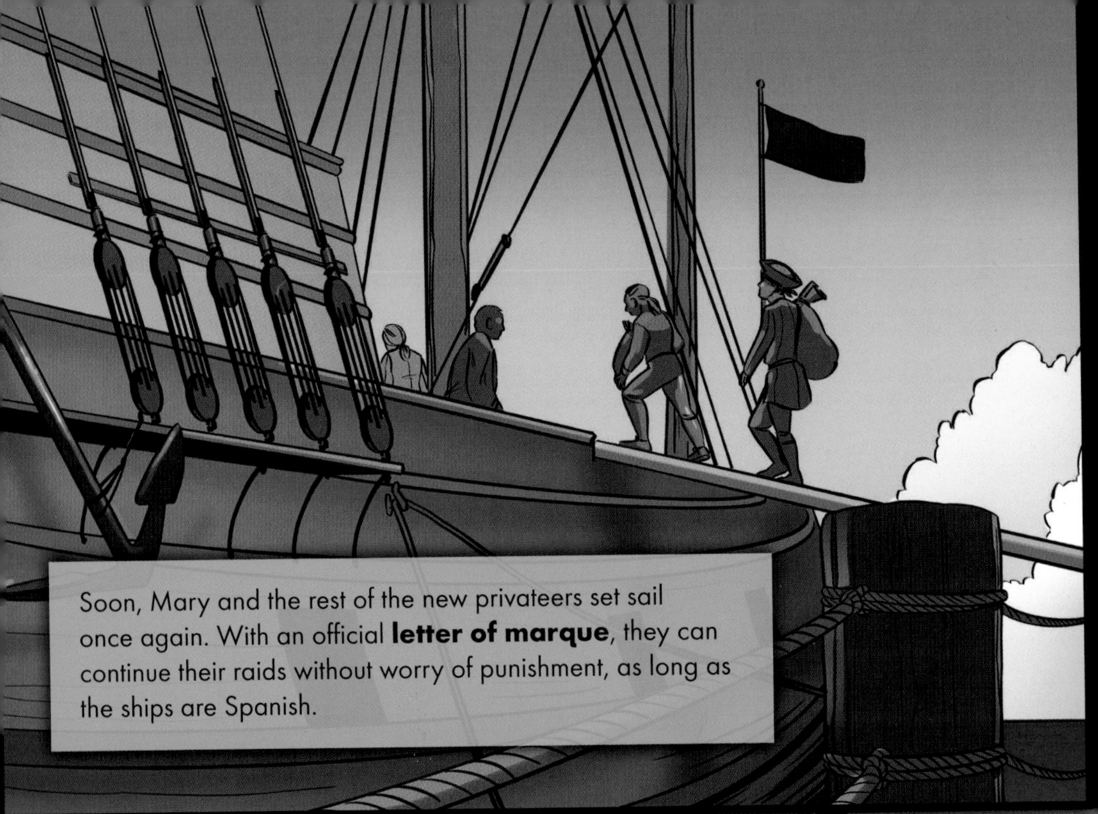
Soon, Mary and the rest of the new privateers set sail once again. With an official **letter of marque**, they can continue their raids without worry of punishment, as long as the ships are Spanish.

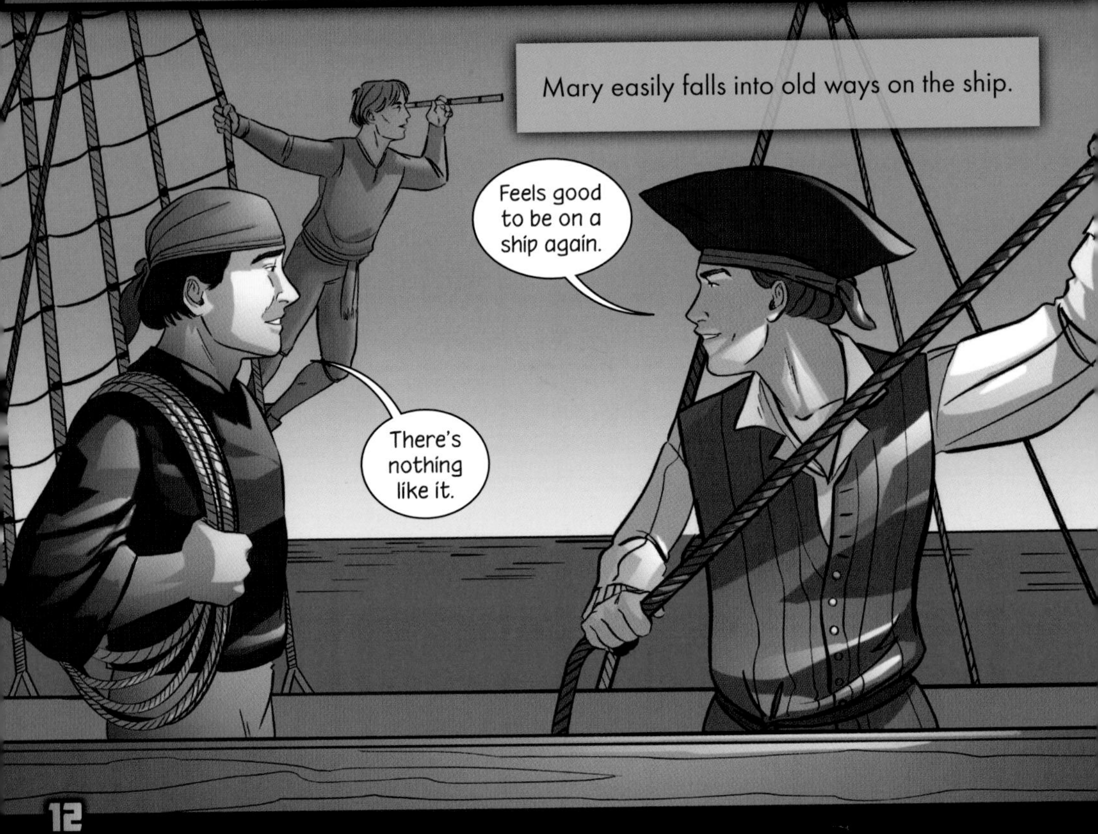
Mary easily falls into old ways on the ship.
Feels good to be on a ship again.
There's nothing like it.

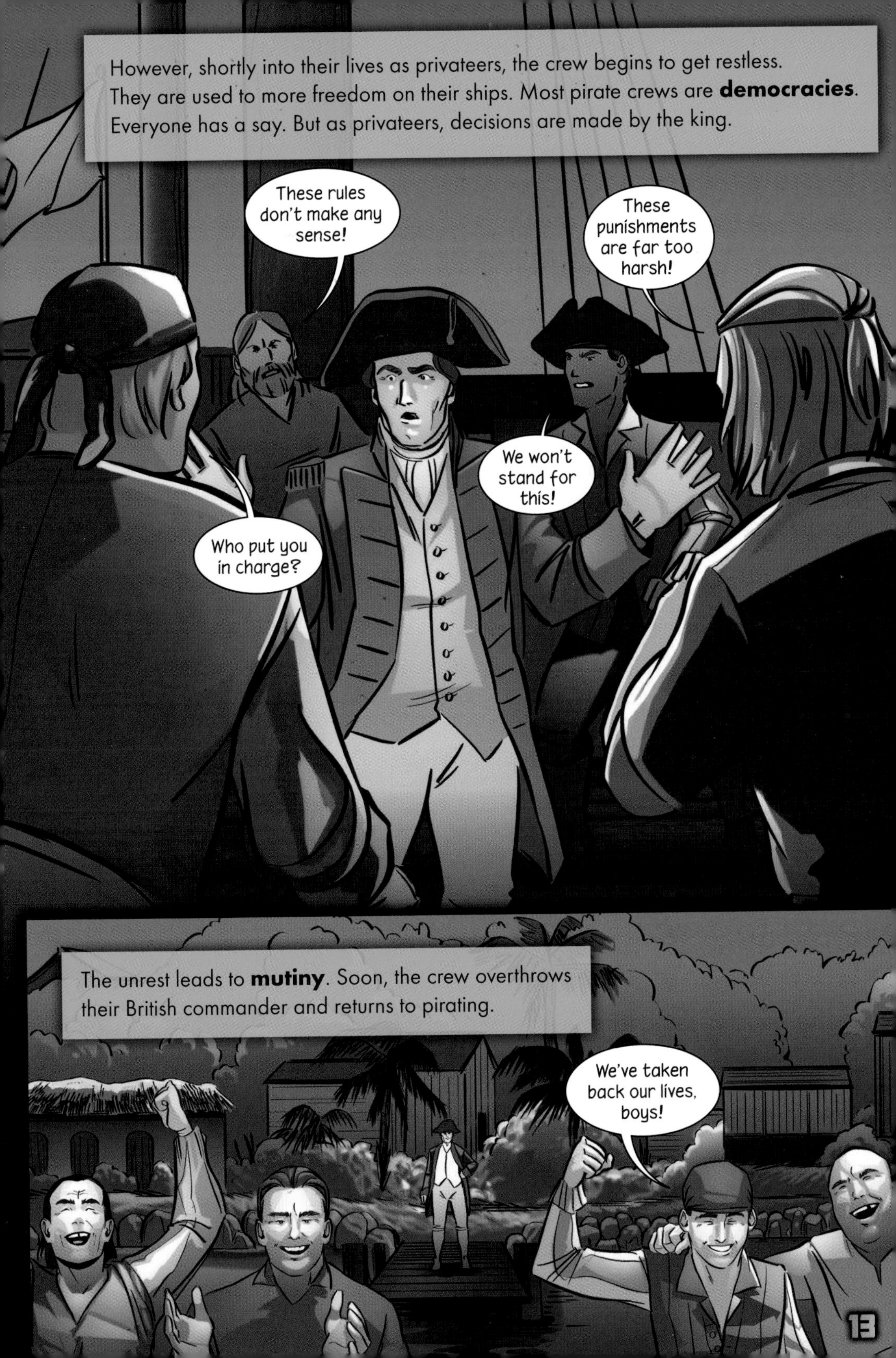
However, shortly into their lives as privateers, the crew begins to get restless. They are used to more freedom on their ships. Most pirate crews are **democracies**. Everyone has a say. But as privateers, decisions are made by the king.
These rules don't make any sense!
These punishments are far too harsh!
We won't stand for this!
Who put you in charge?
The unrest leads to **mutiny**. Soon, the crew overthrows their British commander and returns to pirating.
We've taken back our lives, boys!

A New Crew

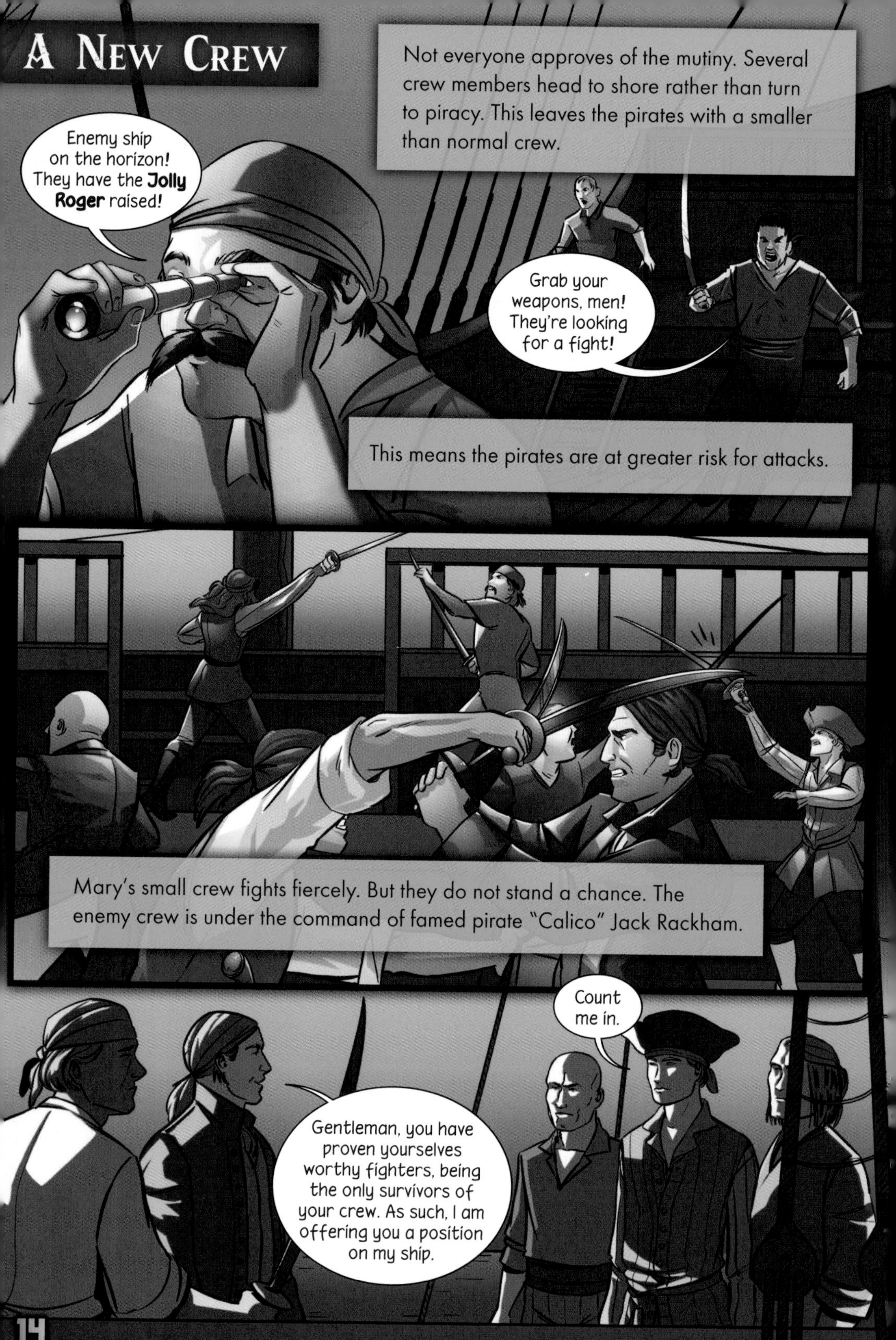

Not everyone approves of the mutiny. Several crew members head to shore rather than turn to piracy. This leaves the pirates with a smaller than normal crew.
Enemy ship on the horizon! They have the **Jolly Roger** raised!
Grab your weapons, men! They're looking for a fight!
This means the pirates are at greater risk for attacks.
Mary's small crew fights fiercely. But they do not stand a chance. The enemy crew is under the command of famed pirate "Calico" Jack Rackham.
Gentleman, you have proven yourselves worthy fighters, being the only survivors of your crew. As such, I am offering you a position on my ship.
Count me in.

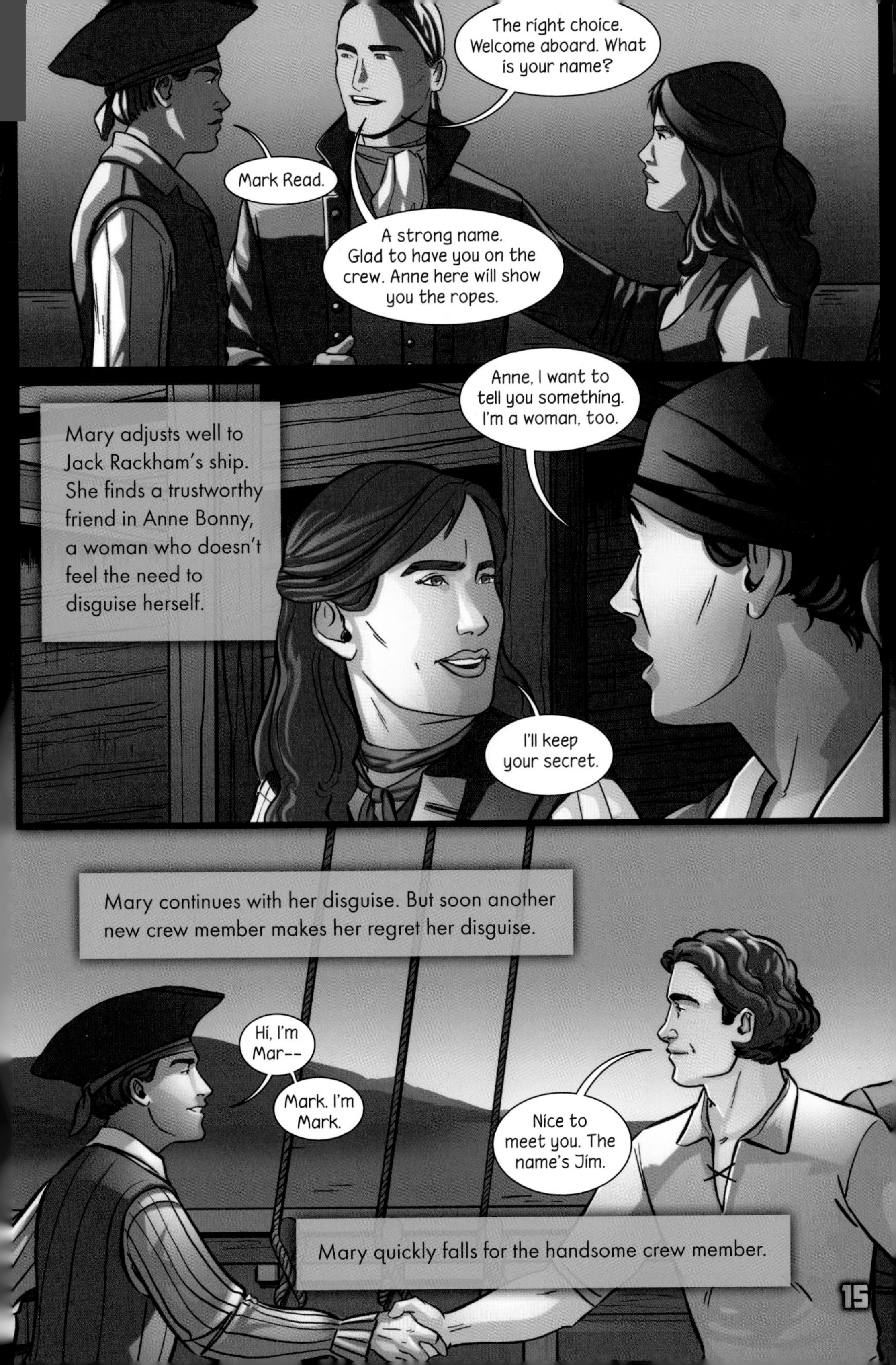

The right choice. Welcome aboard. What is your name?
Mark Read.
A strong name. Glad to have you on the crew. Anne here will show you the ropes.
Mary adjusts well to Jack Rackham's ship. She finds a trustworthy friend in Anne Bonny, a woman who doesn't feel the need to disguise herself.
Anne, I want to tell you something. I'm a woman, too.
I'll keep your secret.
Mary continues with her disguise. But soon another new crew member makes her regret her disguise.
Hi, I'm Mar--
Mark. I'm Mark.
Nice to meet you. The name's Jim.
Mary quickly falls for the handsome crew member.

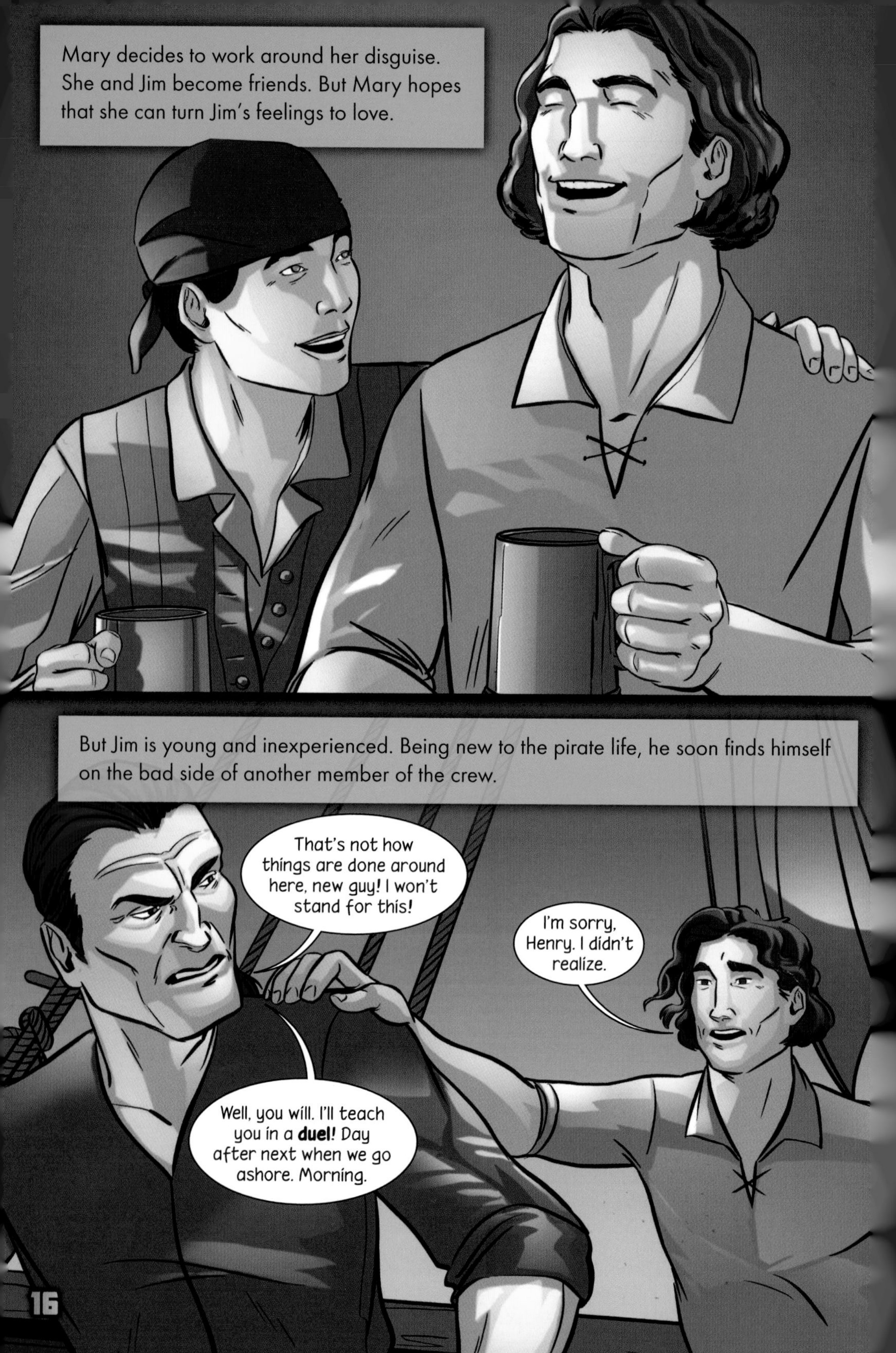
Mary decides to work around her disguise. She and Jim become friends. But Mary hopes that she can turn Jim's feelings to love.
But Jim is young and inexperienced. Being new to the pirate life, he soon finds himself on the bad side of another member of the crew.
That's not how things are done around here, new guy! I won't stand for this!
I'm sorry, Henry. I didn't realize.
Well, you will. I'll teach you in a **duel!** Day after next when we go ashore. Morning.

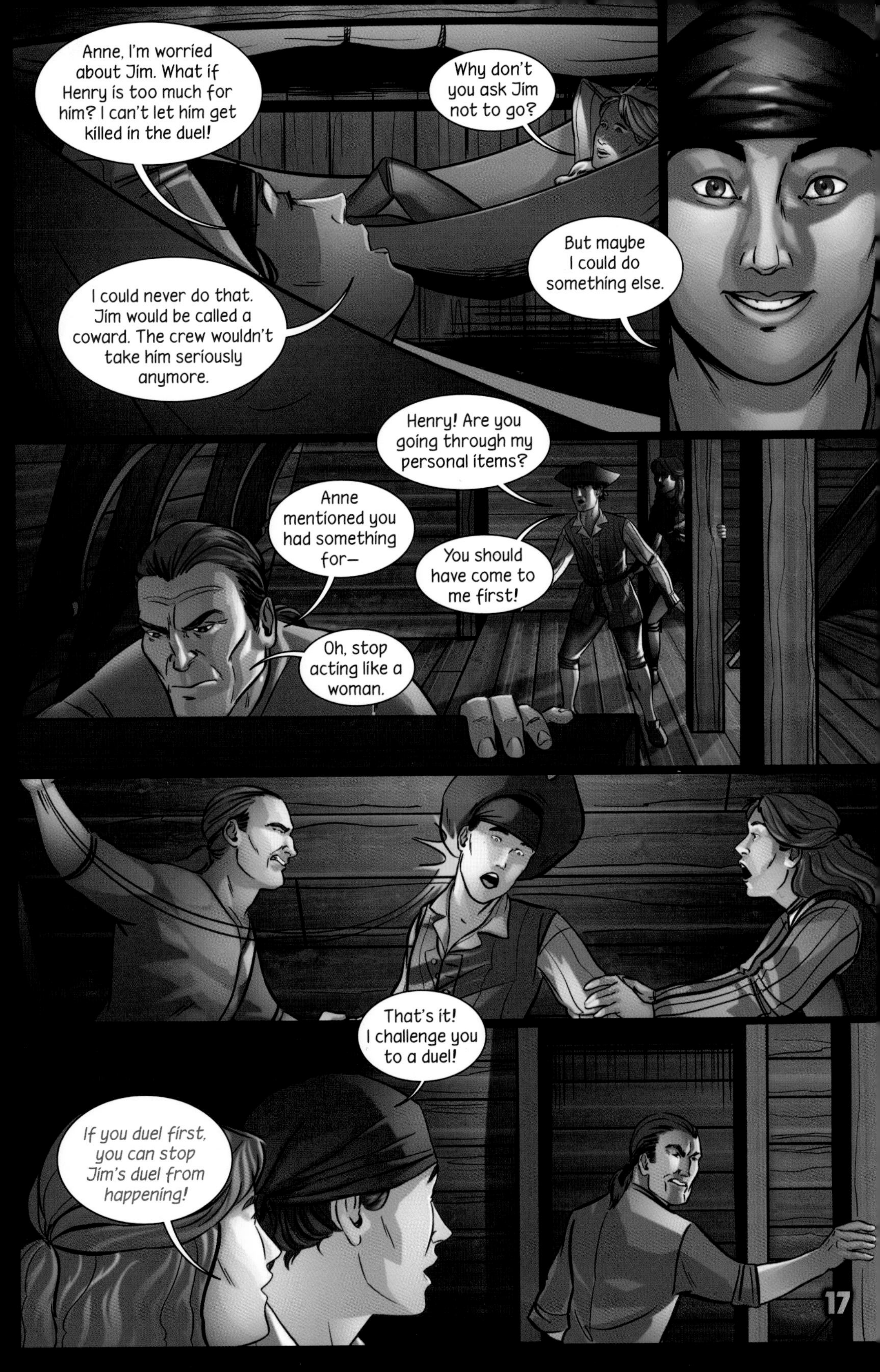
Anne, I'm worried about Jim. What if Henry is too much for him? I can't let him get killed in the duel!
Why don't you ask Jim not to go?
I could never do that. Jim would be called a coward. The crew wouldn't take him seriously anymore.
But maybe I could do something else.
Henry! Are you going through my personal items?
Anne mentioned you had something for—
You should have come to me first!
Oh, stop acting like a woman.
That's it! I challenge you to a duel!
If you duel first, you can stop Jim's duel from happening!

The Duel

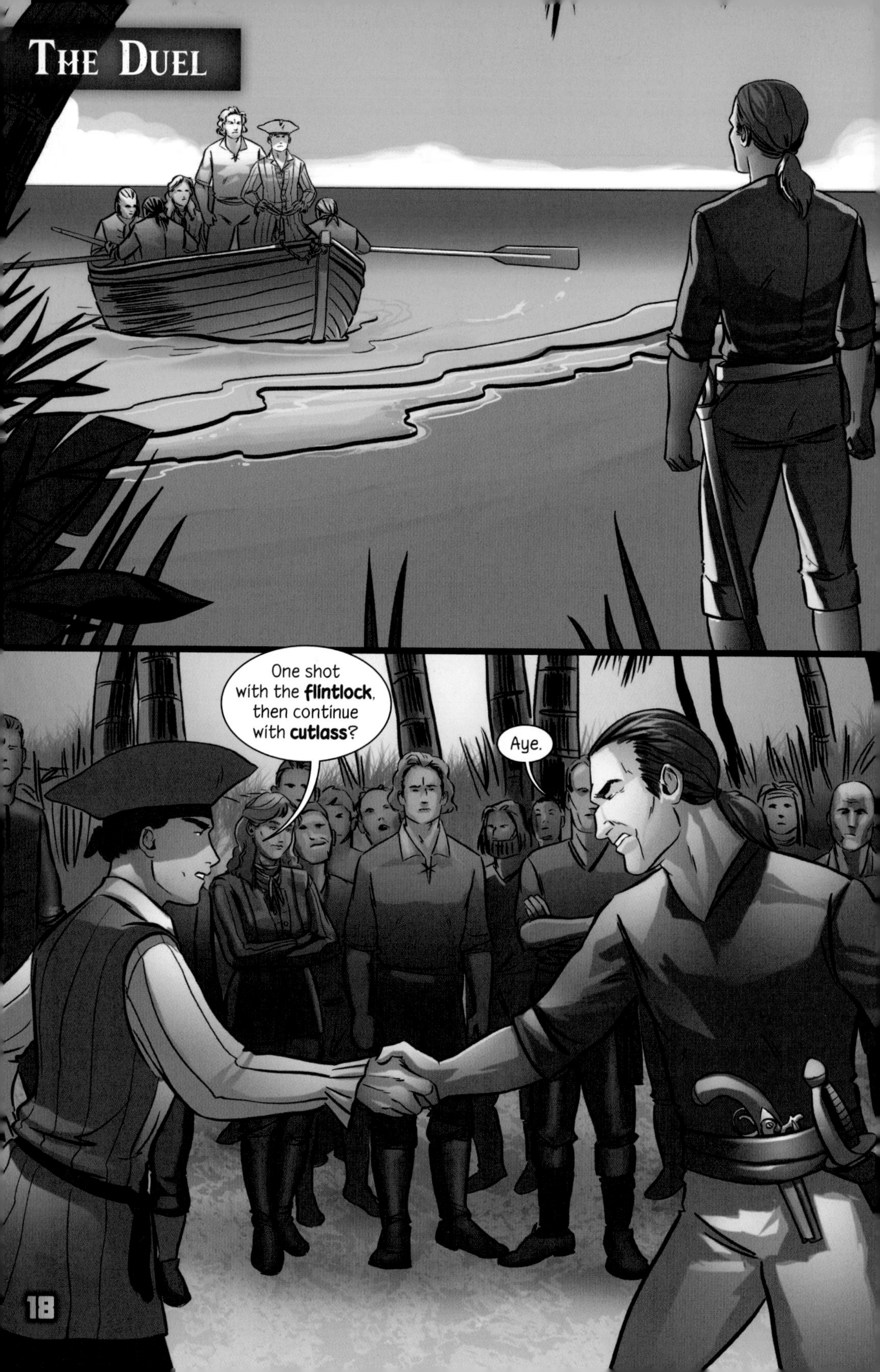
One shot with the flintlock, then continue with cutlass?
Aye.

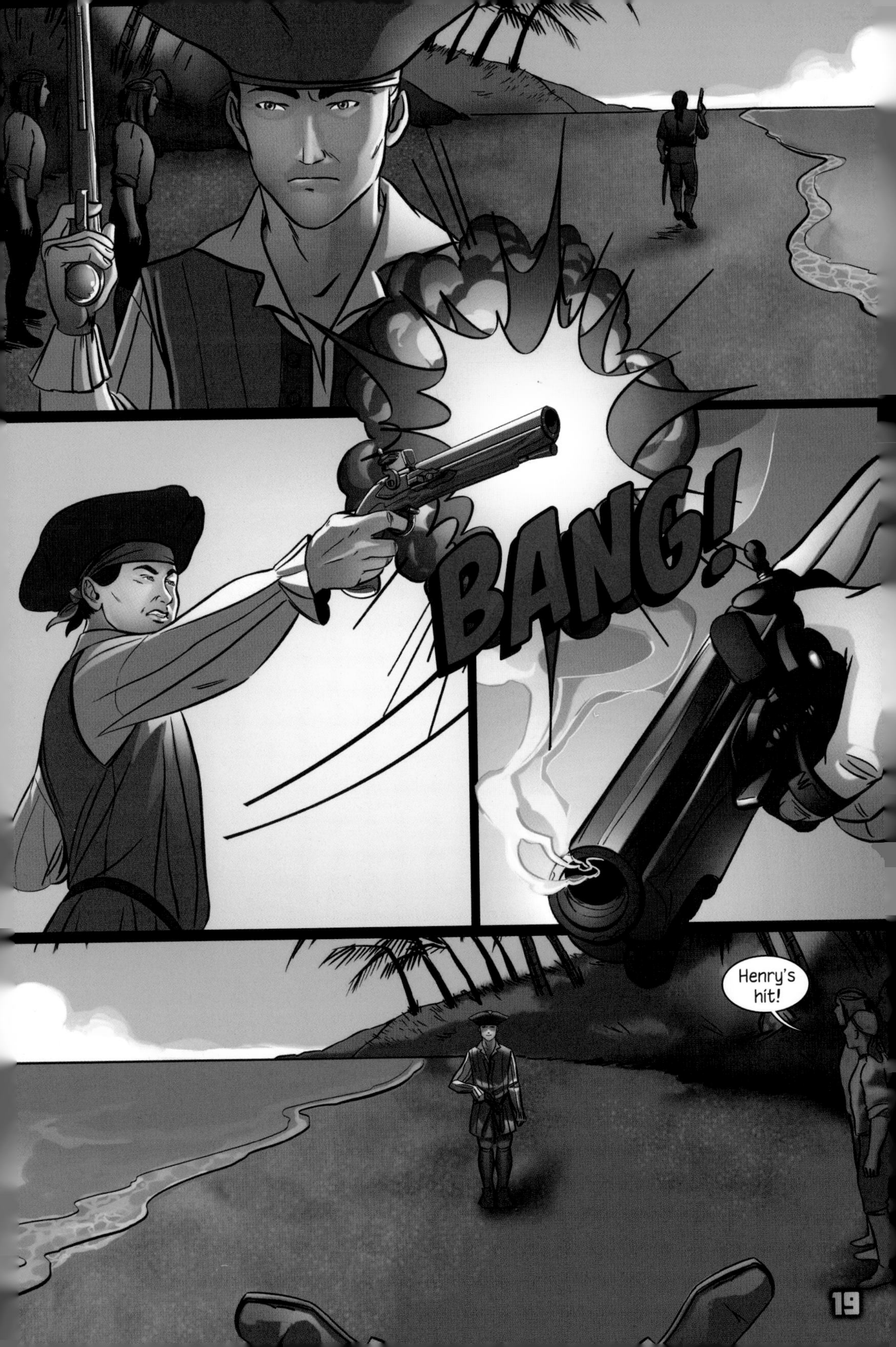
BANG!
Henry's hit!

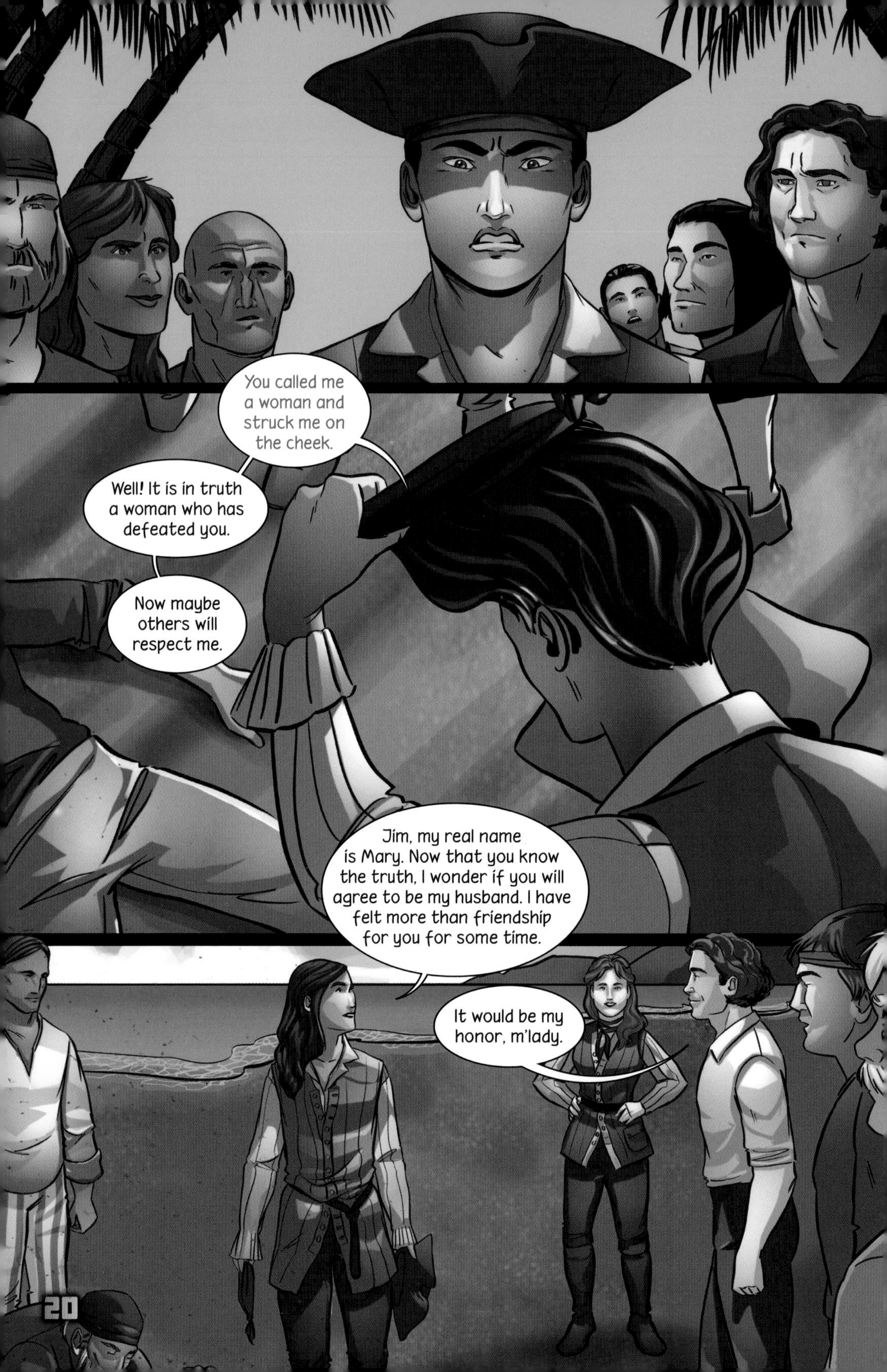
You called me a woman and struck me on the cheek.
Well! It is in truth a woman who has defeated you.
Now maybe others will respect me.
Jim, my real name is Mary. Now that you know the truth, I wonder if you will agree to be my husband. I have felt more than friendship for you for some time.
It would be my honor, m'lady.

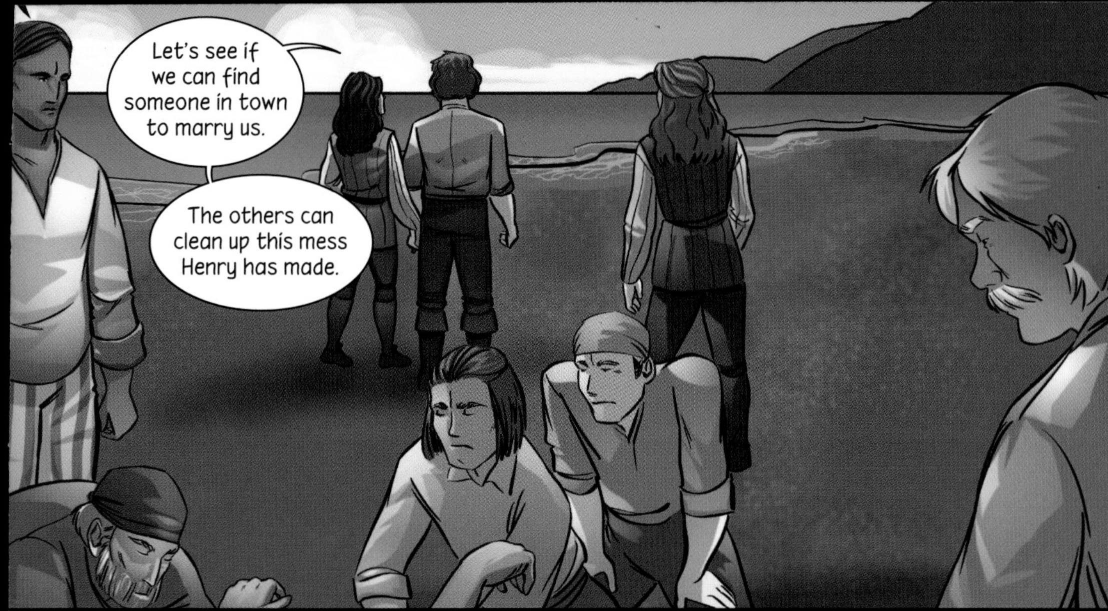
Let's see if we can find someone in town to marry us.
The others can clean up this mess Henry has made.

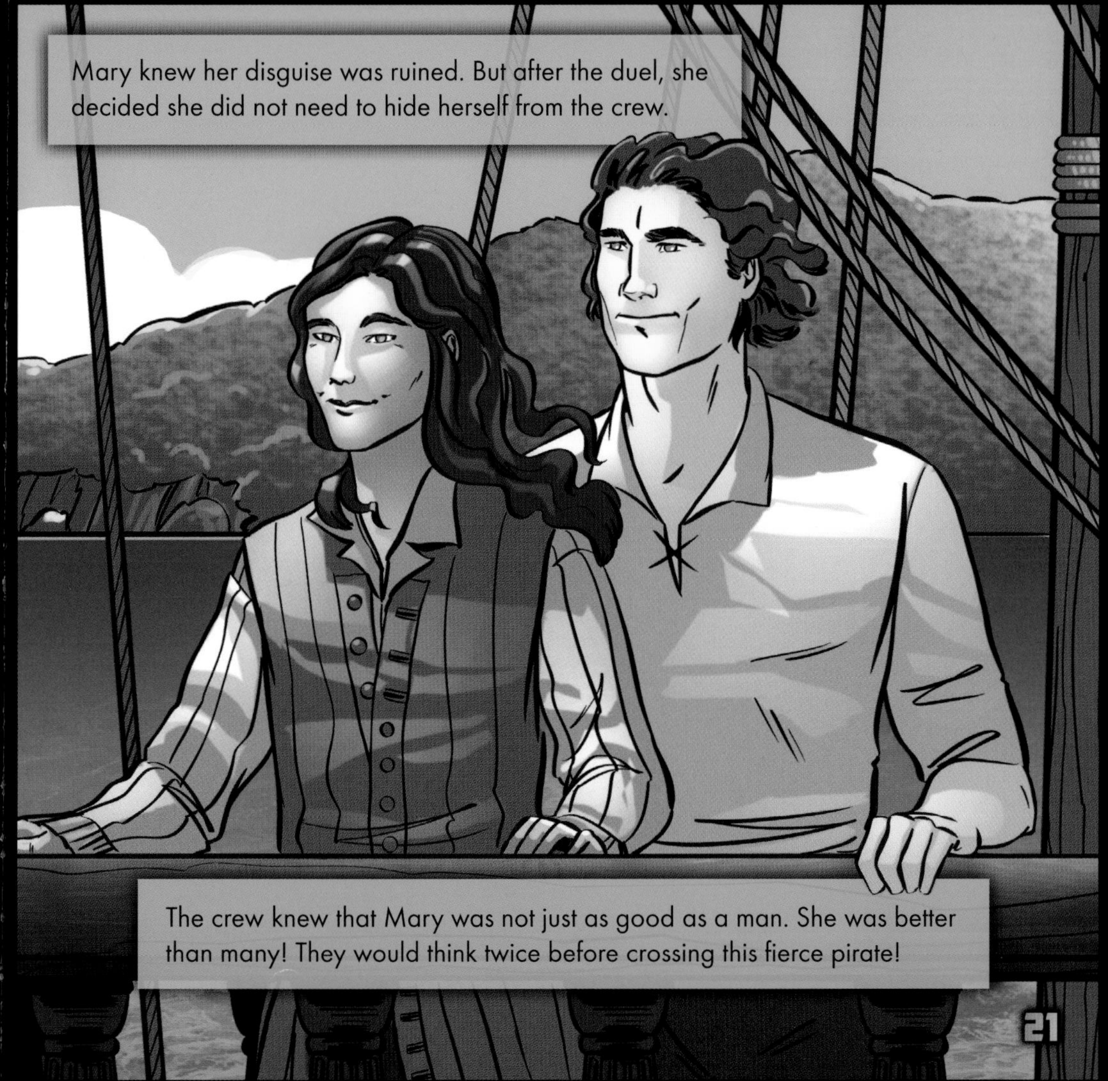
Mary knew her disguise was ruined. But after the duel, she decided she did not need to hide herself from the crew.
The crew knew that Mary was not just as good as a man. She was better than many! They would think twice before crossing this fierce pirate!

More About Mary Read

- Soon after Mary's duel, the crew stole a British ship called the *William*. The crew was then captured and sentenced to death However, Mary's punishment was delayed because she was pregnant. She is believed to have died in prison.
- Stories say Mary saved her husband's life again during her trial. She refused to reveal his identity. Because of this, he was able to say that he was forced into piracy, and they let him go!
- Sources say Mary was involved in as many as 17 duels!

Timeline

around 1713: Mary's first husband dies

around 1714: Mary leaves Europe for the West Indies

1718: Mary and her pirate crew accept the king's pardon, only to return to piracy shortly after

1720: Mary duels with another pirate to protect her lover

1721: Mary Read is believed to have died in prison for stealing a British ship

Mary Read's Travels

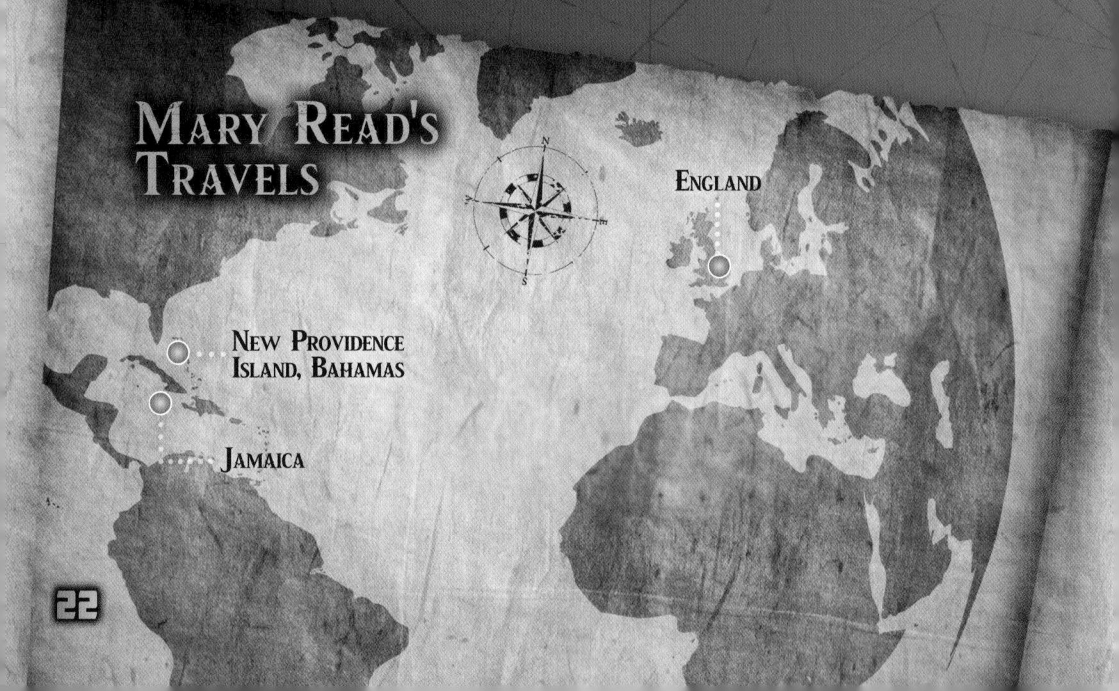
England
New Providence Island, Bahamas
Jamaica

GLOSSARY

cutlass—a short, curved sword

democracies—forms of government or leadership where the people have a say in decisions

duel—a formal fight between two people

flintlock—a pistol fired by creating a spark with flint

Jolly Roger—a black pirate flag with a white skull and crossbones that usually was a warning to nearby ships

letter of marque—a document that gives ships permission to capture enemy merchant ships

mutiny—an uprising against the leadership, especially on a ship

pardon—an official forgiveness of all wrongdoing

plundered—had goods taken by force

pounds—the unit of money for England; pound is short for pound sterling.

privateers—sailors that are licensed to attack enemy ships

raids—surprise attacks that use force

surrender—an act of giving up

wedlock—the state of being married; children born out of wedlock have parents who were unmarried.

West Indies—the islands in the Caribbean Sea; the West Indies are made up of the Bahamas and the Greater and Lesser Antilles.

To Learn More

AT THE LIBRARY

Duncombe, Laura Sooke. *A Pirate's Life for She: Swashbuckling Women Through the Ages*. Chicago, Ill.: Chicago Review Press Incorporated, 2020.

Leaf, Christina. *Anne Bonny: Pirate Queen of the Caribbean*. Minneapolis, Minn.: Bellwether Media, 2021.

Steer, Dugald A. *Pirateology*. Cambridge, Mass.: Candlewick Press, 2006.

ON THE WEB

FACTSURFER

Factsurfer.com gives you a safe, fun way to find more information.

1. Go to www.factsurfer.com
2. Enter "Mary Read" into the search box and click 🔍.
3. Select your book cover to see a list of related content.

INDEX